Timeless Hymns &
Their Stories
(31 Day Devotional)

By Rev. Mark Munter

DEDICATION

I dedicate this book to the Children's Ministry in Alabama called the Adullam House. All proceeds from the sales of this book will go in support of this ministry that houses these kids of incarcerated parents. I also dedicate this book to Bro. Pete and Sis. Angie Spackman who by their faith and love, has been such an inspiration in my life.

Table of Contents

Table of Contents

Introduction

"I remember from the age of four years old sitting on a Church pew at an old-fashioned Pentecostal Church. I remember opening a hymnal that I could not yet read and attempting to sing some of the most beautiful songs I had ever heard. Years later I continue to sing these same songs that I grew up hearing and singing. However, over the years these songs began to have new meaning for me. I began to understand what Jesus did for me on the Cross of Calvary and suddenly these songs began to come alive in my heart. The great hymns of the Church have been sung by countless congregations, for hundreds of years. Although I do believe there are many wonderful contemporary Christian songs, there is nothing quite like singing songs like "Amazing Grace" or "It Is Well With My Soul". My desire in writing this book is to tell the stories behind these timeless hymns. I pray that as you read and sing them, you would understand the stories behind them and the struggles and triumphs of their authors and why we too, can sing and worship through any storm in this life!

"A Mighty Fortress Is Our God"

This famous hymn was written by Martin Luther in 1529 and was later translated from German to English by Frederick H. Hedge in 1852-1853. Several years before this, on October 31, 1517, Martin Luther nailed his famous ninety-five theses (A list of grievances and heretical doctrines of the Catholic Church) to the door of the Cathedral in Wittenberg, Germany. This moment was the spark that would begin the Protestant Reformation. Years later, and under immense persecution, Martin Luther read Psalm 46:1, "God is our refuge and strength, a very present help in trouble." This verse inspired him to think and consider the fact that God is our refuge, shelter, and fortress no matter what the world or Satan throws our way. It is from this verse that this amazing hymn was born and would become the battle cry of the Protestant Reformation. Years later, this hymn has now been translated into virtually every known language and is regarded as one of the greatest examples of Christian hymns.

"A Mighty Fortress Is Our God"

1 A mighty fortress is our God,
  a bulwark never failing;
our helper he, amid the flood
  of mortal ills prevailing.
  For still our ancient foe
  doth seek to work us woe;
his craft and power are great,
and armed with cruel hate,
  on earth is not his equal.

2 Did we in our own strength confide,
  our striving would be losing,
were not the right Man on our side,
the Man of God's own choosing.
  Dost ask who that may be?
  Christ Jesus, it is he;
Lord Sabaoth his name,
from age to age the same;
  and he must win the battle.

"A Mighty Fortress Is Our God"

3 And though this world, with devils
filled, should threaten to undo us,
we will not fear, for God hath willed
his truth to triumph through us.
The prince of darkness grim,
we tremble not for him;
his rage we can endure,
for lo! his doom is sure;
one little word shall fell him.

4 That Word above all earthly powers
no thanks to them abideth;
the Spirit and the gifts are ours
through him who with us sideth.
Let goods and kindred go,
this mortal life also;
the body they may kill:
God's truth abideth still;
his kingdom is forever!

"A Shelter In The Time Of Storm"

Ira David Sankey was just entering his twenties when the American Civil War (1861-1865) began. During this time, he was known to help his unit's Chaplain lead his fellow soldiers in the singing of different hymns as they would pray and worship God. Five years after the war was over, Sankey had become a well-known gospel singer. Then one day while at the local YMCA he met the famous evangelist D.L Moody. Later in October of 1871, while Sankey and Moody were in the middle of a great revival meeting, the Great Chicago Fire began. The two men barely escaped the inferno with their lives. Shortly after, Sankey found a hymn that was written by a man named Vernon J. Charlesworth who was an Elder and Minister at Charles's Surgeon's church in London. It was said to be a favorite song of the fishermen on the north coast of England, and they were often heard singing it as they approached their harbors in "the time of storm". In 1885, fourteen years after the Chicago Fires, Ira Sankey arranged the music and published the famous hymn, "A Shelter In The Time Of Storm".

"A Shelter In The Time Of Storm"

1 The Lord's our Rock, in Him we hide,
    A Shelter in the time of storm;
        Secure whatever ill betide,
    A Shelter in the time of storm.

Chorus:

Oh, Jesus is a Rock in a weary land,
    A weary land, a weary land.
Oh, Jesus is a Rock in a weary land,
    A Shelter in the time of storm.

2 A shade by day, defense by night,
    A Shelter in the time of storm;
No fears alarm, no foes afright,
    A Shelter in the time of storm.

"A Shelter In The Time Of Storm"

3 The raging storms may round us beat,
   A Shelter in the time of storm;
   We'll never leave our safe retreat,
   A Shelter in the time of storm.

Chorus:

Oh, Jesus is a Rock in a weary land,
   A weary land, a weary land.
Oh, Jesus is a Rock in a weary land,
   A Shelter in the time of storm.

4 O Rock divine, O Refuge dear,
   A Shelter in the time of storm;
   Be Thou our Helper ever near,
   A Shelter in the time of storm.

"Alas! And Did My Savior Bleed"

Isaac Watts was born on July 17, 1674, in Southampton, England. He was considered a highly intelligent student and in his latter teen years studied at an Academy with Rev. Thomas Rowe. About eight years later at the age of twenty-four, Watts preached his first sermon and became the assistant minister at the Independent Church he attended. Four years later, he became the Senior Pastor at the Church and continued for many years until his health began to fail. Then in 1707 Isaac Watts published one of his many famous Hymns, "Alas! And Did My Savior Bleed". Almost 150 years later, while in a service at a Methodist Church, the later famous hymn writer Fanny Crosby testified that as she heard this song, she saw how that for so long she still held on to the world with one hand and Jesus with the other. Then and there she made the decision to truly surrender all. In 1885, Ralph Hudson added the famous refrain to the song that we now well know as, "At The Cross".

"Alas! And Did My Savior Bleed"

1 Alas! And did my Savior bleed
and did my Sovereign die?
Would He devote that sacred head
for such a worm as I?

2 Was it for crimes that I had done
He groaned upon the tree?
Amazing pity! Grace unknown!
And love beyond degree!

3 Well might the sun in darkness hide
And shut his glories in,
When Christ, the mighty Maker died,
For man the creature's sin.

4 Thus might I hide my blushing face
While His dear cross appears,
Dissolve my heart in thankfulness,
And melt my eyes to tears.

"Alas! And Did My Savior Bleed"

5 But drops of grief can ne'er repay
The debt of love I owe:
Here, Lord, I give myself away,
'Tis all that I can do.

Chorus:

At the cross, at the cross where I first
saw the light, and the burden of my heart
rolled away. It was there by faith I
received my sight, and now I am happy
all the day!

"All Hail The Power Of Jesus' Name"

Often called "The National Anthem of Christendom", this hymn was written by Edward Perronet and first appeared in the November 1779 issue of the Gospel Magazine published by the writer of "Rock of Ages", Augustus Toplady. Several years later, a missionary named Rev. E. P. Scott came to India to preach the Gospel. One day as he was ministering, he saw on the street a man dressed very oddly. After inquiring about him, he learned that the man belonged to a wild mountain tribe among whom Christ had never been preached. After much prayer, and despite warnings from friends, E.P. Scott decided to visit the tribe. As soon he neared the village, he was suddenly ambushed by a war party. The men surrounded him with their spears ready to thrust him through his heart. E.P. Scott quickly drew out his violin that he always carried with him and began to play and sing in the native language, "All hail the power of Jesus' name!" He closed his eyes, expecting to die at any moment,

"All Hail The Power Of Jesus' Name"

but to his amazement, as he opened his eyes,
the wild men had lowered their spears and
tears were now swelling up in their eyes! E.P.
Scott was then invited to come to their village,
where he would spend the next two years
among them, winning countless of them to
faith in Christ. There is still power in the
mighty name of Jesus!

"All Hail The Power Of Jesus' Name"

1 All hail the power of Jesus' name!
Let angels prostrate fall.
Bring forth the royal diadem,
and crown him Lord of all.
Bring forth the royal diadem,
and crown him Lord of all!

2 Ye chosen seed of Israel's race,
ye ransomed from the fall,
hail him who saves you by his grace,
and crown him Lord of all.
Hail him who saves you by his grace,
and crown him Lord of all!

3 Let every kindred, every tribe,
on this terrestrial ball,
to him all majesty ascribe,
and crown him Lord of all!

"All Hail The Power Of Jesus' Name"

4 Oh, that with yonder sacred throng
we at his feet may fall!
We'll join the everlasting song
and crown him Lord of all.
We'll join the everlasting song
and crown him Lord of all.

"Amazing Grace"

Almost three hundred years ago, a man named John Newton was born in London, England. His earliest memories were of his Godly mother, who despite her failing health, continually devoted herself to prayer and teaching her son the Word of God. Then tragically when John Newton was only seven years old, his mother died after battling tuberculosis for many years. As time passed, Newton became a hardened and cruel man who went from being a crew member and a slave himself to a Captain aboard several different slave ships in England. However, in 1748, while on one of his trips at sea, his ship came into a violent storm that threatened to tear the ship apart and sink it. Out of options and utterly helpless, Newton fell to his knees begging God to have mercy on him and his ship. After several hours, the storm had settled, and this moment would become the turning point in John Newton's life. To everyone's amazement, several years later in 1757, Newton had gone through such a radical transformation, that he began his journey of pursuing full-time ministry.

"Amazing Grace"

After several years of study, he was ordained by the Church of England and became the Pastor of a small Church in Olney, England. Then in 1779, John Newton penned the words to a hymn called "Faith's Review and Expectation", this powerful hymn would later become the most famous hymn of all time, "Amazing Grace."

"Amazing Grace"

1 Amazing grace! How sweet the sound,
that saved a wretch like me!
I once was lost, but now am found,
was blind, but now I see.

2 'Twas grace that taught my heart to
fear and grace my fears relieved;
how precious did that grace appear
the hour I first believed!

3 Through many dangers, toils and
snares I have already come:
'tis grace has brought me safe thus far,
and grace will lead me home.

4 The Lord has promised good to me,
his word my hope secures;
he will my shield and portion be
as long as life endures.

"Amazing Grace"

5 Yes, when this flesh and heart shall fail,
  and mortal life shall cease:
I shall possess, within the veil,
  a life of joy and peace.

6 The earth shall soon dissolve like snow,
  the sun forbear to shine;
but God, who called me here below,
  will be forever mine.

7 When we've been there ten thousand
  years, bright shining as the sun,
We've no less days to sing God's praise
Than when we'd first begun.

"Are You Washed In The Blood?"

Elisha A. Hoffman was born in 1839 in Orwigsburg, Pennsylvania. His father served many years as a minister with the Evangelical Association which undoubtedly influenced Elisha's decision to pursue ministry. After graduating from Union Seminary in Pennsylvania, he married and then later was ordained by the Presbyterian Church. Tragically, after only ten short years of marriage, his wife Susan died leaving him a widower with three sons. Despite this great tragedy, Elisha continued faithfully preaching and ministering the word of God wherever he went. While pastoring at Benton Harbor Presbyterian Church in Michigan, Hoffman composed several hymns born out of his prayer time and devotion to God. During this time, the Lord blessed Elisha with a new wife, who brought great healing and comfort to his heart. Throughout his lifetime Hoffman would go on to write more than 2,000 gospel songs including, "Leaning on the Everlasting Arms", "Glory to His Name" (Down at the Cross), and "I must tell Jesus".

"Are You Washed In The Blood?"

1 Have you been to Jesus for the cleansing power? Are you washed in the blood of the Lamb? Are you fully trusting in His grace this hour? Are you washed in the blood of the Lamb?

Chorus:
Are you washed in the blood?
In the soul-cleansing blood of the Lamb?
Are your garments spotless? Are they white as snow? Are you washed in the blood of the Lamb?

2 Are you walking daily by the Savior's side? Are you washed in the blood of the Lamb? Do you rest each moment in the Crucified? Are you washed in the blood of the Lamb?

"Are You Washed In The Blood?"

3 When the Bridegroom cometh will
your robes be white? Are you washed in
the blood of the Lamb? Will your soul be
ready for the mansions bright,
and be washed in the blood of the
Lamb?

4 Lay aside the garments that are stained
with sin, and be washed in the blood of
the Lamb; There's a fountain flowing for
the soul unclean, O be washed in the
blood of the Lamb!

"Blessed Assurance"

Perhaps one of the greatest female hymn writers of all time was a woman by the name of Frances Jane Crosby, or as she was more commonly known as, Fanny Crosby. She was born on March 24th, 1820, in the city of Brewster, New York. Tragically, at only six weeks old, Fanny became blind, due to a poor decision by a doctor who applied an improper treatment to her eyes while she had a cold. As a child, Crosby was raised by her mother and her grandmother who taught her practical things about the world around her but placed the greatest emphasis on knowing and memorizing God's word. Then at the age of fifteen, Crosby was accepted into the New York Institution for the Blind, where she received her education. Several years later, Fanny would become a teacher in the same institution. She was a gifted and compassionate teacher and taught other blind children in courses on American History and English Grammar. Then in 1858, she married a fellow teacher named Alexander Van Alstyne, who was blind as well. Tragedy struck again a year later when their child that

"Blessed Assurance"

was born died in infancy. It is believed that Crosby's hymn "Safe in the Arms of Jesus" was inspired by her child's death. As the years went by, despite her blindness and many difficulties she had to overcome, Fanny Crosby would go on to write over 8,000 hymns. Besides the hymn "Blessed Assurance" which was published in 1873, many of Crosby's other hymns were also published in over 900 different hymnal books, across all denominational lines. The most famous being hymns like: "Draw Me Nearer", "He Hideth My Soul", "Near the Cross", "Pass Me Not, O Gentle Savior", "Praise Him! Praise Him!", "Redeemed, How I Love to Proclaim It!", "Tell Me the Story of Jesus", and "To God Be the Glory".

"Blessed Assurance"

1 Blessed assurance, Jesus is mine!
Oh, what a foretaste of glory divine!
Heir of salvation, purchase of God,
born of his Spirit, washed in his blood.

Chorus:
This is my story, this is my song,
praising my Savior all the day long.
This is my story, this is my song,
praising my Savior all the day long.

2 Perfect submission, perfect delight,
visions of rapture now burst on my sight.
Angels descending bring from above
echoes of mercy, whispers of love.

3 Perfect submission, all is at rest.
I in my Savior am happy and blessed,
watching and waiting, looking above,
filled with his goodness, lost in his love.

"Bringing In The Sheaves"

Knowles Shaw was born near New London, Ohio, on the 13th of October 1834. His early life was spent in Rush County, Indiana, where he first began to play the violin. In the coming years, he would supply the music for many dance parties. One evening while playing for a rowdy dance party, Shaw began to feel convicted and ceased playing right in the middle of the piece he was performing. All eyes watched in amazement as he packed his violin up and left, never to return there again. After surrendering his life to Christ, Shaw decided to use his talents that he once used for the world, to lead others to Jesus. Upon entering Ministry full-time, Knowles traveled from West to South preaching and leading worship services. Some records kept at that time suggest that the Lord used Shaw to bring nearly 20,000 people to Christ. As he traveled, he quickly became known as the "singing evangelist." Although most of his songs are largely unknown to the masses, the final one he wrote in 1874, shortly before his tragic death in a railroad accident, is well known and can still be found in many a hymnal.

"Bringing In The Sheaves"

1 Sowing in the morning, sowing seeds of kindness, Sowing in the noontide and the dewy eve; Waiting for the harvest, and the time of reaping, We shall come rejoicing, bringing in the sheaves.

Chorus:

Bringing in the sheaves, bringing in the sheaves, We shall come rejoicing, bringing in the sheaves, Bringing in the sheaves, bringing in the sheaves, We shall come rejoicing, bringing in the sheaves.

2 Sowing in the sunshine, sowing in the shadows, Fearing neither clouds nor winter's chilling breeze; By and by the harvest, and the labor ended, We shall come rejoicing, bringing in the sheaves.

"Bringing In The Sheaves"

3 Going forth with weeping, sowing for
the Master, Though the loss sustained
our spirit often grieves; When our
weeping's over, He will bid us welcome,
We shall come rejoicing, bringing in the
sheaves.

Chorus:

Bringing in the sheaves, bringing in the
sheaves, We shall come rejoicing,
bringing in the sheaves, Bringing in the
sheaves, bringing in the sheaves, We
shall come rejoicing, bringing in the
sheaves.

"Come, Thou Fount of Every Blessing"

Robert Robinson was born in Swaffham, Norfolk, in 1735. Tragically as a boy, Robinson lost his father and his widowed mother was consequently left completely impoverished. Unable to provide for him any longer she sent him at the age of 14 years old to be apprenticed to a barber/hairdresser in London. However, his instructor quickly found that Robinson preferred reading to his actual work. One evening at the age of 17, Robinson, with a few of his friends, attended a George Whitefield meeting with the sole purpose of ridiculing him. However, as the man of God preached his message on "The Wrath To Come", Robinson became deeply convicted and surrendered his life to Christ. A few years later he entered the ministry as a Methodist preacher but only for a few years as he would later join the Baptist denomination and Pastor in Cambridge, England. At the age of 23, he penned his most famous hymn, "Come, Thou fount of every blessing"

"Come, Thou Fount of Every Blessing"

1 Come, thou Fount of every blessing,
tune my heart to sing thy grace;
streams of mercy, never ceasing,
call for songs of loudest praise.
Teach me some melodious sonnet,
sung by flaming tongues above.
Praise the mount I'm fixed upon it,
mount of thy redeeming love.

2 Here I raise my Ebenezer:
Here by Thy great help I've come;
And I hope, by Thy good pleasure,
Safely to arrive at home.
Jesus sought me when a stranger,
Wand'ring from the fold of God;
He, to rescue me from danger,
Interposed His precious blood.

"Come, Thou Fount of Every Blessing"

3 O to grace how great a debtor
Daily I'm constrained to be!
Let Thy goodness, like a fetter,
Bind my wandering heart to Thee.
Prone to wander, Lord, I feel it,
Prone to leave the God I love;
Here's my heart, O take and seal it,
Seal it for Thy courts above.

"Come Unto Me"

Charles Price Jones was born in December of 1865, near Rome, Georgia. He grew up attending a Baptist church but was not converted until he was 19 years old while living in Arkansas. A year later, he felt the call to ministry and began preaching. He would go on to Pastor several Baptist churches throughout his lifetime. One day after praying and asking God for a deeper experience of his grace, Jones experienced a closeness with God he had never felt. From this deepened relationship he penned another of his famous hymns, "Deeper, Deeper". His determination to walk with God was evident every day, and he was continually inspired to write many songs including another of his famous hymns, "I Would Not Be Denied". As he preached, he never lost sight of the Savior drawing him and saying to him and to all, "Come unto Me!" Jones became dissatisfied with the state of his Church and began to teach and emphasize the doctrine of holiness within the Baptist church. He faced much opposition from some of the members, both from his congregation and from other Baptist churches as well. Eventually, those who supported him voted to remove the name "Baptist" from the Church and change it to the "Church of Christ." This led to the eventual founding of the Church of Christ (Holiness) U.S.A.

"Come Unto Me"

1 Hear the blessed Savior calling the oppressed, "Oh, ye heavy-laden, come to Me and rest; Come, no longer tarry, I your load will bear, Bring Me every burden, bring Me every care."

Chorus:
Come unto Me, I will give you rest; Take My yoke upon you, hear Me and be blessed; I am meek and lowly, come and trust My might; Come, My yoke is easy, and My burden's light.

2 Are you disappointed, wandering here and there, dragging chains of doubt and loaded down with care? Do unholy feelings struggle in your breast? Bring your case to Jesus—He will give you rest.

"Come Unto Me"

3 Stumbling on the mountains dark with sin and shame, stumbling toward the pit of hell's consuming flame; By the powers of sin deluded and oppressed, Hear the tender Shepherd, "Come to Me and rest."

4 Have you by temptation often conquered been, has a sense of weakness brought distress within? Christ will sanctify you, if you'll claim His best; In the Holy Spirit, He will give you rest.

"Count Your Blessings"

Johnson Oatman Jr. is the perfect example of a hard-working man used by God. He was born in Medford, New Jersey in April of 1856. His father owned and operated a mercantile business which his son would later join adding to the name, "Johnson Oatman & Son". After his father's death, Oatman would change his career to work selling life insurance which he would do for the next 15 years of his life. During this time, he preached on and off at his local Church but felt he was not gifted enough to Pastor. He felt his calling lied elsewhere, and in his thirties, he found it in writing song lyrics. Oatman worked hard at his insurance job until he was promoted to administrator. However, during his spare time, he continually wrote new hymns including his four most famous ones: "Count Your Blessings", "Higher Ground", "No Not One", and "The Hallelujah Side". Johnson Oatman Jr would go on to write an incredible five thousand hymns for the Church. His life proved you can be used for God no matter what your occupation is. He is only looking for a willing vessel.

"Count Your Blessings"

1 When upon life's billows you are tempest tossed. When you are discouraged, thinking all is lost. Count your many blessings, name them one by one, and it will surprise you what the Lord hath done.

Chorus:
Count your blessings, name them one by one. Count your blessings, see what God has done! Count your blessings, name them one by one, and it will surprise you What the Lord has done.

2 Are you ever burdened with a load of care? Does the cross seem heavy you are called to bear? Count your many blessings, every doubt will fly, and you will keep singing as the days go by.

"Count Your Blessings"

3 When you look at others with their lands and gold. Think that Christ has promised you His wealth untold. Count your many blessings money cannot buy. Your reward in Heaven, nor your home on high.

4 So, amid the conflict whether great or small. Do not be disheartened, God is over all. Count your many blessings, Angels will attend, help and comfort give you to your journey's end.

"God Will Take Care Of You"

This beloved hymn was written in 1904, by Civilla D. Martin. It was composed while the Martins were spending several weeks as guests at a Bible School in Lestershire, New York. Their purpose in being there was to help the president of the school compose a new songbook. Civilla's husband, Rev. W. Stillman Martin, was a well-known Baptist evangelist. One Sunday morning, he was invited to preach at a church that was a good distance from the Bible school. Before they could leave, however, Civilla became very ill. Rev. Martin seriously considered canceling his preaching engagement, but just before he did, his son spoke up and said, "Father, don't you think that if God wants you to preach today, He will take care of mother while you are away?" Agreeing with the wisdom of his young son, Martin decided to leave and trust God for his wife, while he was gone. The service proved to be powerfully anointed and blessed by God, with several people turning to Christ for Salvation. Returning later that evening, Martin found that while he was gone, Civilla had written a new hymn inspired by the remark of

"God Will Take Care Of You"

their young son earlier that day. That same evening, Rev. Martin composed the music for his wife's words and added it to the songbook that he was preparing. A short time later, the Martins befriended an older couple named the Doolittles. The wife had been bedridden for twenty long years. Her husband was himself in a wheelchair. Yet despite their afflictions, they had a continual peace and joy of the Lord in their lives. One day while visiting them, Rev. Martin asked Mrs. Doolittle what the secret was to their continual joy. Mrs. Doolittle simply replied, "His eye is on the sparrow, and I know He watches me." This so influenced Civilla that it inspired another of her well-known hymns, "I sing because I'm happy, I sing because I'm free, for His eye is on the sparrow, and I know He watches me." This song along with her first hymn, "God Will Take Care of You" shows the importance of our continual trust in God. We can know that no matter what we face, he will always take care of us!

"God Will Take Care Of You"

1 Be not dismayed whate'er betide, God will take care of you; Beneath His wings of love abide, God will take care of you.

Chorus:
God will take care of you, through every day, o'er all the way; He will take care of you, God will take care of you.

2 Through days of toil when heart doth fail, God will take care of you; When dangers fierce your path assail, God will take care of you.

3 All you may need He will provide; God will take care of you; Nothing you ask will be denied, God will take care of you.

4 No matter what may be the test, God will take care of you; Lean, weary one, upon His breast, God will take care of you.

"Great Is Thy Faithfulness"

Thomas Chisolm was born in Franklin, Kentucky in 1866. He grew up being educated in a small country school where he would later become a teacher at. He excelled at writing and at the age of 21 he became the editor of a local weekly newspaper in Franklin. In his mid-twenties, Chisolm came under the ministry of Dr. Henry Clay Morrison who was influential in leading him to the Lord. In 1903, Thomas Chisolm was ordained with the Methodist Church and began Pastoring in Kentucky. However, over the years, due to poor health, Chisolm moved his family and had to work a variety of other jobs to make ends meet. However, during this time he penned hundreds of hymns, and by the end of his life, he will have written over 1,200. In his own words, he did not write the hymn, "Great Is Thy Faithfulness" because of any big or specific event in his life; but rather as a reflection of God's everyday faithfulness and care throughout his entire life. As the word of God says continually, "God is faithful!"

"Great Is Thy Faithfulness"

1 Great is thy faithfulness, O God my
Father, there is no shadow of turning
with thee. Thou changest not, thy
compassions, they fail not; as thou hast
been, thou forever wilt be.

Chorus:
Great is thy faithfulness! Great is thy
faithfulness! Morning by morning new
mercies I see; all I have needed thy hand
hath provided. Great is thy faithfulness,
Lord, unto me!

2 Summer and winter and springtime
and harvest, sun, moon, and stars in their
courses above, join with all nature in
manifold witness to thy great faithfulness,
mercy, and love.

"Great Is Thy Faithfulness"

3 Pardon for sin and a peace that endureth, thine own dear presence to cheer and to guide, strength for today and bright hope for tomorrow, blessings all mine, with ten thousand beside!

Chorus:
Great is thy faithfulness! Great is thy faithfulness! Morning by morning new mercies I see; all I have needed thy hand hath provided. Great is thy faithfulness, Lord, unto me!

"Have Thine Own Way, Lord"

Adelaide A. Pollard loved the Lord with all her heart and her one desire since she was born again was to be used by the Lord to reach the lost. She set out in her early forties to raise funds to go to the mission field in Africa. However, after each year went by, Adelaide became more and more disheartened at the lack of funding she was able to raise. Discouraged and confused one night she attended a local prayer meeting. While seeking the Lord she heard an elderly woman pray these words, "It's all right, Lord. It doesn't matter what you bring into our lives, just have your own way with us." That night at home, she contemplated not only the prayer but also the story of the potter from Jeremiah 18:3, "Then I went down to the potter's house, and there he was, making something at the wheel." The realization hit her that she was the clay, not the potter and that what the Lord wanted most from her, was to yield to the potter's hands. Inspired by God's word and the woman's prayer she penned the words of this hymn, "Have Thine Own Way, Lord!"

"Have Thine Own Way, Lord"

1 Have Thine own way, Lord! Have Thine own way! Thou art the Potter, I am the clay. Mold me and make me after Thy will, While I am waiting, yielded and still.

2 Have Thine own way, Lord! Have Thine own way! Search me and try me, Master, today! Whiter than snow, Lord, wash me just now, As in Thy presence humbly I bow.

3 Have Thine own way, Lord! Have Thine own way! Wounded and weary, help me, I pray! Power, all power, surely is Thine! Touch me and heal me, Savior divine.

4 Have Thine own way, Lord! Have Thine own way! Hold o'er my being absolute sway! Fill with Thy Spirit till all shall see Christ only, always, living in me.

"He Giveth More Grace"

Annie Johnson Flint was born to Eldon and Jean Johnson on Christmas Eve in 1866. However tragically, before she reached the age of six, both of her parents died within a few short years of each other. Annie and her sister were adopted by a kind, childless couple who raised them and brought them regularly to a local Baptist Church. At the tender young age of 8, Annie recalled being in the service and being moved upon by the Holy Spirit. She gave her heart to Jesus that night. After high school, she spent a year training to become a teacher and took a position close to home. However, in her second year of teaching, she began to develop severe arthritis. Her condition steadily worsened until it became difficult for her to walk at all. She gave up teaching and had to use a wheelchair to get around. Shortly after both of her adoptive parents died within months of each other, leaving Annie and her sister alone again. She relied heavily on God's promises and the verse, "My grace is sufficient for you, for my strength is made perfect in weakness."

"He Giveth More Grace"

Instead of complaining, she came to say, like the Apostle Paul, "Therefore most gladly I will rather boast in my infirmities, that the power of Christ may rest upon me… For when I am weak, then I am strong." Though she suffered many tragic losses she never became bitter towards God, but rather trusted him even more for strength and grace to get through every trial. She penned the words to this hymn and the others she wrote from a place of brokenness and trust in God.

"He Giveth More Grace"

1 He giveth more grace when the burdens grow greater, He sendeth more strength when the labors increase; To added afflictions, He addeth His mercy, To multiplied trials, His multiplied peace.

2 When we have exhausted our store of endurance when our strength has failed ere the day is half done, when we reach the end of our hoarded resources our Father's full giving is only begun.

3 Fear not that thy need shall exceed His provision, Our God ever yearns His resources to share; Lean hard on the arm everlasting, availing; The Father both thee and thy load will upbear.

"He Giveth More Grace"

4 His love has no limits, His grace has no measure, His power no boundary known unto men; For out of His infinite riches in Jesus He giveth, and giveth, and giveth again.

"He Keeps Me Singing"

Luther B. Bridgers grew up going to revival meetings where his father Rev. James Bridgers would often preach. As Luther grew older, he started assisting his father in the meetings and began preaching himself as a teenager. While attending Asbury College in Wilmore, Kentucky, he met his future wife Sarah Jane Veatch with whom he later had three sons. After graduating, Luther was ordained as a minister with the Methodist Church and began Pastoring for a short while before following in his father's footsteps and doing itinerant Evangelism. During this time, he wrote his famous Hymn, "He Keeps Me Singing". However, circumstances a year later would test his heart if he could indeed keep on singing and worshipping God. Luther accepted an invitation to minister at a conference in Kentucky. However, due to the traveling distance, he had to leave his family in the care of his father-in-law. In Kentucky, Luther had two wonderful weeks of revival in which many were saved and delivered. The last night he closed the services out and was informed he had a phone call. Expecting to

"He Keeps Me Singing"

hear his wife on the phone, Luther instead was shocked as he received the tragic news that a fire had burned down his father-in-law's house and had killed him and Luther's wife and 3 children. Although brokenhearted by the tragic loss of his family, Luther Bridgers did in fact 'keep singing'. In fact, his ministry and evangelism only intensified as he preached the word of God and was able to minister to others who had also gone through similar tragic circumstances. What the enemy had tried to destroy him with, God turned around and used to bring many souls into the kingdom of God. Luther not only ministered all throughout the United States but was also able to do missions work in Belgium, Czecho-slovakia, and Russia. Till his dying day, he kept singing and preaching the good news that Jesus saves!

"He Keeps Me Singing"

1 There's within my heart a melody Jesus whispers sweet and low, Fear not, I am with thee, peace, be still, In all of life's ebb and flow. Jesus, Jesus, Jesus, Sweetest Name I know, fills my every longing, keeps me singing as I go.

2 All my life was wrecked by sin and strife, Discord filled my heart with pain, Jesus swept across the broken strings, Stirred the slumbering chords again. Jesus, Jesus, Jesus, Sweetest Name I know, fills my every longing, keeps me singing as I go.

3 Feasting on the riches of His grace, resting 'neath His sheltering wing, always looking on His smiling face, that is why I shout and sing. Jesus, Jesus, Jesus, Sweetest Name I know, fills my every longing, keeps me singing as I go.

"He Keeps Me Singing"

4 Though sometimes He leads through waters deep, Trials fall across the way, Though sometimes the path seems rough and steep, See His footprints all the way. Jesus, Jesus, Jesus, Sweetest Name I know, fills my every longing, keeps me singing as I go.

5 Soon He's coming back to welcome me, far beyond the starry sky, I shall wing my flight to worlds unknown, I shall reign with Him on high. Jesus, Jesus, Jesus, Sweetest Name I know, fills my every longing, keeps me singing as I go.

"He Leadeth Me"

Dr. Joseph H. Gilmore was born in April of 1834 in Boston, Massachusetts. In his late twenties, during the height of the Civil War, Joseph preached on a regular basis at the First Baptist Church in Philadelphia, PA. One Sunday morning as he was preaching from the 23rd Psalm, he suddenly stopped as he read the verse, "He leadeth me… beside still waters." These words gripped Joseph to the core, even in the midst of the dark days of the Civil War, God was still leading his people. Joseph preached his entire message that day filling the congregation's heart with hope because of the simple fact, 'he leadeth us'. After the service, After the service Dr. Gilmore and his wife were invited to the Deacon's home for a time of food and fellowship, while there, Dr. Gilmore sat at the table pondering the words, "He Leadeth Me". He then took out a piece of paper and unknowingly wrote what would be the words to a new famous hymn. He handed the paper to his wife, who unbeknownst to her husband sent the words off to a weekly Christian magazine in Boston called *The Watchman*

"He Leadeth Me"

and *The Reflector*. Joseph had forgotten about the poem and a few years later he and his wife tried out for a new Pastorate at a Baptist Church in Rochester, NY. Before service, he picked up a hymnal to see what songs the Church was singing, and to his surprise, his hymn, which he had written three years earlier had been published and was now being sung in worship by the congregation. He truly does lead us, and as a preacher friend I know once said, "We are better led than we know."

"He Leadeth Me"

1 He leadeth me, O blessed thought!
O words with heavenly comfort fraught!
Whate'er I do, where'er I be, still 'tis
God's hand that leadeth me.

Chorus:
He leadeth me, He leadeth me,
By His own hand He leadeth me;
His faithful follower I would be,
For by His hand He leadeth me.

2 Sometimes 'mid scenes of deepest
gloom, Sometimes where Eden's bowers
bloom, By waters still, o'er troubled sea,
Still 'tis His hand that leadeth me.

3 Lord, I would place my hand in Thine,
Nor ever murmur nor repine; Content,
whatever lot I see, Since 'tis my God that
leadeth me.

"He Leadeth Me"

4 And when my task on earth is done,
When by Thy grace the victory's won,
Even death's cold wave I will not flee,
Since God through Jordan leadeth me.

Chorus:
He leadeth me, He leadeth me,
By His own hand He leadeth me;
His faithful follower I would be,
For by His hand He leadeth me.

"He Lives"

Alfred Henry Ackley was born in Spring Hill, Pennsylvania in 1887. Early on his father began to teach him music and soon Alfred became a talented and well-known musician who played the piano and the cello. After graduating from Westminster Theological Seminary in Maryland he was ordained as a Presbyterian minister. He ministered all over the United States and even worked with famed evangelist Billy Sunday for a few years. One day while Ackley was preaching an evangelistic crusade, a young Jewish student bluntly asked, "Why should I worship a dead Jew?" Ackley energetically replied, "Because he lives! I tell you, He is not dead, but lives here and now! Jesus Christ is more alive today than ever before. I can prove it by my own experience, as well as the testimony of countless thousands." Later that same evening after hearing the powerful testimony of the risen Savior, the Jewish young man gave his heart, not to a dead Jew, but to a living Christ! Ackley sat down at a piano and penned the words he preached so fervently, "He Lives!"

"He Lives"

1 I serve a risen Savior, He's in the world today; I know that He is living, whatever men may say; I see His hand of mercy, I hear His voice of cheer, and just the time I need Him He's always near.

Chorus:
He lives, He lives, Christ Jesus lives today! He walks with me, and He talks with me, along life's narrow way.
He lives, He lives, salvation to impart!
You ask me how I know He lives:
He lives within my heart.

2 In all the world around me I see His loving care, and though my heart grows weary I never will despair; I know that He is leading thro' all the stormy blast, The day of His appearing will come at last.

"He Lives"

3 Rejoice, rejoice, O Christian, lift up your voice and sing, eternal hallelujahs to Jesus Christ the King! The hope of all who seek Him, the help of all who find, None other is so loving, so good and kind.

Chorus:
He lives, He lives, Christ Jesus lives today! He walks with me, and He talks with me, along life's narrow way. He lives, He lives, salvation to impart! You ask me how I know He lives: He lives within my heart.

"His Way With Thee"

Rev. Cyrus Nusbaum was born in 1861 in Middlebury, Indiana. In his mid-twenties, Cyrus was ordained as a Methodist minister and began Preaching and served in many capacities from being a pastor and an evangelist to becoming an Army captain, in World War I and working as an American Red Cross inspector. Early on while Pastoring, Cyrus was assigned to a circuit of several Churches and was paid such a low salary that his family was barely able to survive. After a year of this, Cyrus and his wife attended their denomination's Annual Minister's Conference and hoped to receive a new assignment by the end of it. However, to their dismay, on the last night of the conference, the presiding bishop announced that they would continue their current assignment. Discouraged and disappointed the Nusbaums returned to their lodging and Cyrus stayed up late into the night trying to pray. However, around midnight he finally collapsed to his knees and prayed, "Lord I am willing to serve, regardless of the cost." With that sincere surrender, a supernatural peace came over him.

"His Way With Thee"

1 Would you live for Jesus, and be always pure and good? Would you walk with Him within the narrow road? Would you have Him bear your burden, carry all your load? Let Him have His way with thee.

Chorus:
His power can make you what you ought to be; His blood can cleanse your heart and make you free; His love can fill your soul, and you will see, 'Twas best for Him to have His way with thee.

2 Would you have Him make you free, and follow at His call? Would you know the peace that comes by giving all? Would you have Him save you, so that you need never fall? Let Him have His way with thee.

"His Way With Thee"

3 Would you in His kingdom find a place
of constant rest? Would you prove Him
true in providential test? Would you in
His service labor always at your best?
Let Him have His way with thee.

Chorus:
His power can make you what you ought
to be; His blood can cleanse your heart
and make you free; His love can fill your
soul, and you will see, 'Twas best for
Him to have His way with thee.

"How Great Thou Art"

The following Hymn has perhaps the most unique origins of all. One day a young Swedish minister named Rev. Carl Boberg was walking home from Church in the pouring down rain. As he walked the two miles home, a loud and tempestuous thunderstorm gripped his attention. He watched with amazement as the storm thundered with such might that he quaked in fear at the sound of it. However, there was a certain beauty about it as well. The storm was simply a display of God's power and greatness. When Carl arrived at home he sat down and penned a poem in Swedish called, "O Store Gud" ("O Mighty God") which was published in 1886. More than forty years later, an English missionary named Stuart Hine, heard the song while ministering in Russia. He and his wife preached all over Russia, Czechoslovakia, and Romania, ministering to countless people including those living in the Carpathian Mountains. One day while ministering in a village in the mountains a storm came and thundered loudly, rolling through the mountain range. This reminded

"How Great Thou Art"

Hine of the beautiful Russian hymn translated from the Swedish poem, that he had heard earlier. With fresh inspiration, Hine translated the verses into English, he himself adding lines from his own experience and thus forming the wonderful, completed hymn we know today. "How Great Thou Art" became widely known in 1957 when the Billy Graham Crusades began to sing it regularly in their meetings all around the world. It is regarded today as one of the most popular hymns ever written.

"How Great Thou Art"

1 Oh Lord, my God, when I, in awesome wonder, consider all the worlds Thy hands have made. I see the stars; I hear the rolling thunder. Thy power throughout the universe displayed.

Chorus:
Then sings my soul, my Savior God to Thee. How great Thou art, how great Thou art. Then sings my soul, my Savior God to Thee. How great Thou art, how great Thou art!

2 When through the woods and forest glades I wander, and hear the birds sing sweetly in the trees. When I look down, from lofty mountain grandeur and hear the brook and feel the gentle breeze.

"How Great Thou Art"

3 And when I think that God, His Son not sparing, Sent Him to die, I scarce can take it in. That on the cross, my burden gladly bearing. He bled and died to take away my sin!

Chorus:
Then sings my soul, my Savior God to Thee, how great Thou art, how great Thou art. Then sings my soul, my Savior God to Thee, how great Thou art, how great Thou art!

4 When Christ shall come, with shout of acclamation, and take me home, what joy shall fill my heart. Then I shall bow, in humble adoration, and there proclaim, my God, how great Thou art!

"I Have Decided to Follow Jesus"

Perhaps one of the most challenging and heartbreaking hymns was written not by the man who originated it, but by those that heard him in his final moments before his death. It is greatly debated who actually penned the written words, but the verbal inspiration was from a man from India named Nokseng. He, along with his family, came to faith through the efforts of several Baptist missionaries. The region they were in was known as Assam and was comprised of hundreds of tribes who were primitive and aggressive head hunters. Nokseng himself began to preach and many villagers began to accept Christ as a result. However, this enraged the village chief, and one day he summoned all the villagers. He then called Nokseng and his family and demanded they renounce their faith or face public execution. Moved by the Holy Spirit Nokseng replied: "I have decided to follow Jesus." Enraged at his refusal, the chief ordered his archers to shoot Nokseng's children. As both boys lay dead on the ground in a pool of blood, the chief asked, "Will you deny your faith now? You have lost both your

"I Have Decided to Follow Jesus"

children. You will lose your wife too." But Nokseng replied, "Though none go with me, still I will follow." The chief then ordered his wife to be shot as well. The Chief asked for the last time, "I will give you one more opportunity to deny your faith and live." In the face of death, with tears in his eyes, Nokseng said, "The world behind me, the cross before me. No turning back." He too was then shot dead. The whole village stood in silence and then suddenly tears began to flow down the chief's face. He was convicted by the Holy Spirit and saw a man who was willing to give his life and the life of his family to follow Jesus. The Chief weepingly shouted, "I too believe in Jesus!" in a matter of moments the entire village was weeping, and by the end of the day, all of them too decided to follow Jesus. Nokseng and his family's sacrifice although heartbreaking, was used by God to win not only that village but countless others as well. "And they overcame him by the blood of the Lamb, and by the word of their testimony, and they did not love their lives even unto death." Revelation 12:11

"I Have Decided to Follow Jesus"

1 I have decided to follow Jesus.
I have decided to follow Jesus.
I have decided to follow Jesus.
No turning back, no turning back.

2 Though' none go with me, I still will follow. Though none go with me I still will follow. Though none go with me, I still will follow. No turning back, no turning back.

3 The world behind me, the cross before me. The world behind me, the cross before me. The world behind me, the cross before me. No turning back, no turning back.

"I Have Decided to Follow Jesus"

4 My cross I'll carry, till I see Jesus.
My cross I'll carry till I see Jesus.
My cross I'll carry till I see Jesus.
No turning back, No turning back.

5 Will you decide now to follow Jesus?
Will you decide now to follow Jesus?
Will you decide now to follow Jesus?
No turning back, no turning back.

"I Would Rather Have Jesus"

Although popularized by Christian singer George Beverly Shea, the actual lyrics of this hymn were written much earlier by a woman named Rhea F. Miller in 1922. Rhea was married for a short while to Dr. H.V Miller who was the General Superintendents of the Church of The Nazarene. However, he suddenly passed away one day leaving Rhea a widow. Although she was heartbroken by his passing she was determined to still minister where she could. Her gifting was always in music and combined with her kind and patient demeanor she made an excellent music teacher. She would teach the piano on a regular basis, especially to minister's kids, so they could serve in their local Church with their parents. Rhea continually prayed for her father, who had been a horrible drunk for some time. He would drink and then steal money from his wife's purse, just to go to the bar to drink some more. Mrs. Ross, her mother, was a Godly woman who despite difficulty at home still made it to Church each Sunday. She would walk to church in every kind of weather, be it rain, snow, or shine.

"I Would Rather Have Jesus"

Eventually, through prayer and her living her faith out, her love for the Lord broke through to her husband. He fully surrendered his life to the Lord and was wonderfully delivered from his life of sin. One evening while at Church, he began to share his testimony, and exclaimed, "I'd rather have Jesus than all the gold or silver in the whole world! I'd rather have Him than anything this world has to offer!" Rhea Miller sat in amazement as she heard her father's life-changing testimony and from it, she was inspired to write the words of this powerful hymn, "I would rather have Jesus!"

"I Would Rather Have Jesus"

1 I'd rather have Jesus than silver or gold.
I'd rather be His than have riches untold.
I'd rather have Jesus than houses or lands.
I'd rather be led by His nail-pierced hand.

Chorus:
Then to be the king of a vast domain
Or be held in sin's dread sway.
I'd rather have Jesus than anything
This world affords today.

2 I'd rather have Jesus than men's
applause. I'd rather be faithful to His dear
cause. I'd rather have Jesus than
worldwide fame. I'd rather be true to His
holy name

3 He's fairer than lilies of rarest bloom.
He's sweeter than honey from out the
comb; He's all that my hungering spirit
needs. I'd rather have Jesus and let Him
lead.

"I Will Sing Of My Redeemer"

Philip P. Bliss was born in Clearfield County, PA in 1838. He left home at a very early age and made a living working on farms while trying to continue his education. At the age of twelve, during a revival meeting, Bliss gave his heart to Jesus. He continued studying and developing his gifting in music and before long became an itinerant music teacher. His first hymn was published in 1864, and in 1868 famous preacher D.L. Moody advised him to become a singing evangelist. For the last few years of his life, Bliss traveled with his wife leading music at revival meetings throughout the United States. Philip had a great passion for the Lord and wrote many hymns including one about God's word and the beauty of it called, "Wonderful Words of Life". One evening while ministering in Chicago, Bliss commented to the congregation, "I may not pass this way again", after which he closed the service out with the hymn, "I'm Going Home Tomorrow." Little did he know this would be his final meeting before going to be with the Lord. The next day he and his wife boarded a train back to Pennsylvania. There was a

"I Will Sing Of My Redeemer"

terrible snowstorm and as the train was crossing over a bridge into Ashtabula, Ohio, the bridge suddenly gave way and all the passenger cars fell into the ravine below. Bliss escaped through a window, only to find that his wife was still in the wreckage. Although the train was on fire, Philip was determined to rescue his wife. He forced his way back into the train wreckage but sadly perished while searching for his beloved wife. Among his belongings were found the lyrics to a previously unpublished hymn, "I Will Sing of My Redeemer". Years later it became one of the first songs ever to be recorded on Thomas Edison's new invention, the phonograph.

"I Will Sing Of My Redeemer"

1 I will sing of my Redeemer and his wondrous love to me. On the cruel cross he suffered, from the curse to set me free.

Chorus
Sing, oh, sing of my Redeemer, with His blood He purchased me; on the cross He sealed my pardon. Paid the debt and made me free.

2 I will tell the wondrous story, how my lost estate to save, In His boundless love and mercy, He the ransom freely gave.

3 I will praise my dear Redeemer, His triumphant power I'll tell, How the victory He giveth over sin, and death, and hell.

"I Will Sing Of My Redeemer"

4 I will sing of my Redeemer, And His heavenly love to me; He from death to life hath brought me, Son of God with Him to be.

Chorus
Sing, oh, sing of my Redeemer, with His blood He purchased me; on the cross He sealed my pardon. Paid the debt and made me free.

"In the Garden"

Charles Austin Miles was born in Lakehurst, New Jersey in 1868. As a young man, he attended the Philadelphia College of Pharmacy and subsequently pursued a career as a pharmacist. However, in 1892, after much prayer, he felt led to quit his job at the pharmacy and begin writing gospel music instead. He found a job working at the Hall-Mack Publishing Company, where he would work for the next thirty-seven years. One day in April of 1912, while reading the twentieth chapter of the Gospel of John, Miles began to picture the scene unfold in his mind. He saw it like a vision; the garden, the tomb, Mary weeping, and then Jesus, the resurrected Christ standing there. For Charles, it was as if he himself were there in the garden too. He saw Mary kneeling at the master's feet and crying out, 'Rabboni!' Under the inspiration of this powerful vision, Miles wrote of his experience as if he too were in the garden with him.

"In the Garden"

1 I come to the garden alone,
while the dew is still on the roses.
And the voice I hear, falling on my ear
The Son of God discloses.

Chorus
And He walks with me, and He talks
with me. And He tells me I am His own.
And the joy we share as we tarry there,
None other has ever known.

2 He speaks and the sound of His voice
Is so sweet the birds hush their singing
And the melody that He gave to me
Within my heart is ringing.

3 I stayed in the garden with Him,
Though the night all around me is falling.
But He bids me go, through the voice of
woe, His voice to me is calling.

"It Is Well With My Soul"

Horatio G. Spafford was a successful lawyer and businessman in the city of Chicago, Illinois for many years. He was also an active member of the Presbyterian Church and served as the director and trustee of the Presbyterian Theological Seminary. He and his family were also longtime supporters of the revival evangelist D.L Moody. Horatio Spafford and his wife had to endure many a tragedy throughout the years, beginning in 1870 with the tragic passing of their four-year-old son due to scarlet fever. The following year, in 1871, during the "Great Chicago Fire" Horatio's real estate properties that he had invested in were completely destroyed. However, the greatest tragedy of all occurred in 1873, when Horatio decided to take his family on a vacation trip to England. The trip was intended to not only provide some much-needed time away but also to help assist the Rev. D.L Moody in his upcoming revival services. However, on the day of their departure, Horatio had some last-minute business he had to attend to, so he sent the rest of his family on ahead, planning to follow

"It Is Well With My Soul"

them on another ship in a few days. Mrs. Spafford and her four daughters boarded the French ocean liner the S.S *Ville du Havre*. However, four days into crossing the Atlantic, their ship was suddenly struck by another ship and quickly began to sink. Mrs. Spafford quickly brought her children to the deck and prayed that God would spare them or help them to endure whatever awaited them. Within 12 minutes the S.S *Ville du Havre* sank to the bottom of the ocean. All four of Horatio's daughters drowned leaving only his wife as a survivor in the tragedy that claimed over 200 lives. His wife was found floating on some wreckage and was rescued and brought the rest of the way to England. After arriving in Wales, Mrs. Spafford wired her husband, "Saved alone." When word reached Horatio, he quickly set sail for England to be with his wife. When the ship he was on passed the place where his daughters had drowned, Horatio began to write the words to this powerful hymn, "…When sorrows like sea billows roll. Whatever my lot, thou hast taught me to say, it is well, it is well with my soul."

"It Is Well With My Soul"

1 When peace, like a river, attendeth my way. When sorrows like sea billows roll. Whatever my lot, thou hast taught me to say, it is well, it is well with my soul.

Chorus:
It is well with my soul.
It is well, it is well with my soul.

2 Though Satan should buffet, though trials should come, let this blest assurance control, That Christ hath regarded my helpless estate, and hath shed His own blood for my soul.

3 My sin oh the bliss of this glorious thought! My sin, not in part but the whole, is nailed to the cross, and I bear it no more! Praise the Lord, praise the Lord, O my soul!

"It Is Well With My Soul"

4 For me, be it Christ, be it Christ hence
to live: If Jordan above me shall roll, no
pang shall be mine, for in death as in life,
thou wilt whisper thy peace to my soul.

5 But, Lord, 'tis for Thee, for Thy
coming we wait, The sky, not the grave,
is our goal; Oh, trump of the angel! Oh,
voice of the Lord! Blessed hope, blessed
rest of my soul!

6 And Lord, haste the day when the faith
shall be sight, The clouds be rolled back
as a scroll; The trump shall resound, and
the Lord shall descend, even so, it is well
with my soul.

"Just As I Am"

Charlotte Elliott from an early age had a great love of poetry, both reading and writing it.

One evening, while at dinner, with some friends she met the famous minister Rev. H.A. César Malan who asked her a deeply probing question, was she a Christian? She considered his question offensive, and replied that she would rather not discuss the question. Rev. Malan apologized and stated that he did not mean to offend her but desired all to come to know the Savior. In the coming days, the question haunted her more and more. Was she in fact a true Christian, or was she just religious? Three weeks later, while visiting a mutual friend, Elliot again encountered the minister. However, this time her heart was open to hearing the Gospel. She told him that ever since he had spoken to her, she had been thinking about his question more and more and that now she wished him to tell her how to come to Christ. "Just come to him as you are!" Rev. Malan said. With these words, she surrendered her life to Jesus Christ. Shortly after inspired by these same words, she wrote her most famous poem, "Just As I Am".

"Just As I Am"

Almost exactly 100 years after her hymn was published, a young man named Billy Graham was in a revival meeting in Charlotte, North Carolina. While the Revival Evangelist Rev. Mordecai Ham was preaching, Billy Graham felt convicted and went forward as the Evangelist gave the altar call. As he walked the aisle to the altar, he recalled vividly the altar song they played "Just As I Am, Without One Plea…" This song would later become the same altar song that Billy Graham would use in his countless crusades all over the world. Millions over the years would come forward as they heard these powerful words.

"Just As I Am"

1 Just as I am, without one plea, but that thy blood was shed for me, and that thou bidst me come to thee, O Lamb of God, I come, I come.

2 Just as I am, and waiting not to rid my soul of one dark blot, to Thee whose blood can cleanse each spot, O Lamb of God, I come, I come.

3 Just as I am, though tossed about, with many a conflict, many a doubt, fightings and fears within, without, O Lamb of God, I come, I come.

4 Just as I am, poor, wretched, blind; Sight, riches, healing of the mind, Yea, all I need in Thee to find, O Lamb of God, I come, I come.

"Just As I Am"

5 Just as I am, thou wilt receive, Wilt
welcome, pardon, cleanse, relieve.
because Thy promise I believe, O Lamb
of God, I come, I come.

6 Just as I am, thy love unknown, hath
broken every barrier down; Now, to be
thine, yea, thine alone, O Lamb of God,
I come, I come.

"Leave It There"

Charles A. Tindley was an African American man born in Maryland in July 1851. Although born to slaves, Charles taught himself to read and write by the age of 17. In his mid-twenties, he moved to Philadelphia, PA with his wife and there began a correspondence course in order to become a Methodist Minister. In the early 1900s, after much study, Tindley became the new Pastor of the Calvary Methodist Episcopal Church in Philadelphia, PA. Pastor Charles became well known as a very dynamic preacher who took an active role in his congregants' lives as well as those in the community. Tindley was able to draw people of all races to his church ministry and by the time of his death, his Church ran over 12,000 people. One day in 1916, a man who was a constant worrier visited Pastor Charles. After listening awhile, the Pastor kindly remarked, "My advice to you is to put all your troubles in a sack, take them to the Lord, and leave them there." After the man left, Pastor Charles began to pray and meditate on it. He then pulled out a piece of paper and wrote perhaps his most famous song, "Leave It There".

"Leave It There"

1 If the world from you withhold of its silver and its gold, and you have to get along with meager fare, just remember, in His Word, how He feeds the little bird. Take your burden to the Lord and leave it there.

Chorus:
Leave it there, leave it there. Take your burden to the Lord and leave it there. If you trust and never doubt, He will surely bring you out. Take your burden to the Lord and leave it there.

2 If your body suffers pain and your health you can't regain, and your soul is almost sinking in despair, Jesus knows the pain you feel, He can save and He can heal. Take your burden to the Lord and leave it there.

"Leave It There"

3 When your enemies assail and your
heart begins to fail, don't forget that
God in heaven answers prayer; He will
make a way for you and will lead you
safely through. Take your burden to the
Lord and leave it there.

4 When your youthful days are gone and
old age is stealing on, and your body
bends beneath the weight of care,
He will never leave you then, He'll go
with you to the end. Take your burden to
the Lord and leave it there.

"Oh, For A Thousand Tongues"

Perhaps the most well-known and prolific hymn writer ever to pick up a pen was Charles Wesley. Charles grew up in a sizeable family and was the youngest of eighteen children. When Charles grew up, he attended Oxford University where he formed a prayer group among his fellow students. John Wesley one of his older brothers later joined and ended up leading the group after a time. The group focused on studying the Bible and living a holy life. Their fellow students would often mock and ridicule them, saying that they were the "Holy Club" or "the Methodists" due to their methodical and detailed way of studying the Bible and applying it to their lives. Whether they knew it or not at the time, this would be the beginning of the founding of the Methodist denomination. In 1735, Charles along with his brother John (now ordained with the Anglican Church), traveled to America to minister in the colonies and to the Native Americans. The trip did not go as expected and there was no interest in their message or in them being there by anyone.

"Oh, For A Thousand Tongues"

Dejected and ashamed they both returned to England the following year. Both John and Charles felt there was something missing. They were religious but had not yet experienced the new birth and a relationship with Jesus Christ. After returning to England, Charles taught English to Moravian Missionary Peter Bohler, who challenged Charles to look at the state of his soul a little more deeply. One evening while ill, Charles began to study the Bible and pray and, in those moments, truly received Christ into his heart by faith. His brother John Wesley was converted a few days later. Together they traveled all over England preaching and telling all who would hear, the good news of the Gospel. Charles in his lifetime was accredited with writing over 6,000 hymns. Some of his other most famous hymns include, "Christ The Lord Is Risen Today", "And Can It Be" and the well-known Christmas Hymn, "Hark! The Herald Angels Sing".

"Oh, For A Thousand Tongues"

1 Oh, for a thousand tongues to sing My great Redeemer's praise. The glories of my God and king, the triumphs of His grace!

2 My gracious Master and my God, assist me to proclaim, to spread through all the earth abroad the honors of Thy name.

3 Jesus! the name that charms our fears, that bids our sorrows cease. 'Tis music in the sinner's ears, 'Tis life, and health, and peace.

4 He breaks the power of canceled sin, He sets the prisoner free; His blood can make the foulest clean; His blood availed for me.

"Oh, For A Thousand Tongues"

5 He speaks, and, listening to His voice, new life the dead receive. The mournful, broken hearts rejoice, the humble poor believe.

6 To God, all glory, praise, and love be now and ever given by saints below and saints above, the church in earth and heaven.

"Revive Us Again"

William Paton Mackay was born in Scotland in 1839. However, at the age of seventeen, he left home to attend the University of Edinburgh to study medicine. As he left his mother gave him a Bible in which she wrote his name and a Bible verse on the inside cover. As he studied at the University, William began to drift further and further away from the way he was raised. He began to drink heavily and even pawned the Bible his mother had given him. Upon graduating he began to work in a hospital emergency room full time. One day a young man was brought into the emergency room. He had fallen off a very tall scaffold and was in serious condition. All Dr. Mackay could do at that point was to try to relieve the young man's pain as much as possible. He did not have any family come, but his property owner showed up and brought him his Bible that he had bought at a pawn shop a few years earlier. When Dr. Mackay would check on the young man, he continually saw him holding the Bible close to his chest and reading it whenever he had the strength for a few moments.

"Revive Us Again"

Although visibly in pain the young man still had an amazing, supernatural peace on his face. One week later, however, the young man died. While the nurses tended to the body of the young man, Dr. Mackay picked up the Bible he had held so close to him and opened up the front cover. To his amazement, the Bible contained his own name and the Bible verse that his mother had inscribed on it, years before. All the pages were well-worn, and many verses had been underlined. Dr. MacKay thought about how this Bible brought comfort to this dying young man. It was the book that enabled him to die with peace and enter heaven with joy in his soul. With a sense of shame, Dr. Mackay began to read some of the Bible verses that were underlined. With tears in his eyes, he prayed for God's forgiveness and that he would restore to him the "joy of thy salvation". It was not long after this personal revival in his soul that he wrote the words for his most famous hymn "Revive Us Again." He quit the medical field and dedicated the rest of his life to preaching the Gospel in Scotland.

"Revive Us Again"

1 We praise Thee, O God! For the Son of Thy love, For Jesus Who died, and is now gone above.

Chorus:
Hallelujah! Thine the glory. Hallelujah! Amen. Hallelujah! Thine the glory. Revive us again!

2 We praise Thee, O God! For Thy Spirit of light. Who hath shown us our Savior and scattered our night.

3 All glory and praise to the Lamb that was slain, Who hath borne all our sins, and hath cleansed every stain.

"Revive Us Again"

4 All glory and praise To the God of all grace, who hast brought us, and sought us, And guided our ways.

5 Revive us again; Fill each heart with Thy love; May each soul be rekindled With fire from above.

Chorus:
Hallelujah! Thine the glory. Hallelujah!
Amen. Hallelujah! Thine the glory.
Revive us again!

"Rock Of Ages"

Augustus Toplady was born into a British Military family in 1740. Tragically Augustus' father was killed in the siege of Carthagena, shortly after the child's birth. Years later, he and his mother moved to Ireland for his education. At the age of sixteen, Augustus was powerfully transformed while attending a revival service not held in a Church, but in a barn. He then dedicated his life to the ministry and a few years later became an ordained minister with the Church of England in 1762. One day while traveling along a gorge he was caught in a terrible rainstorm. He took shelter under a large cleft in the rock while he waited for the storm to pass by. As he waited, he thought about the scriptures in the book of Psalms that continually described God as a rock, a shelter, and a refuge. He found a simple playing card and began to inscribe the initial lyrics to his hymn that would be published in 1776. The cleft in the rock that is believed to have sheltered him is now marked on some maps as simply the "Rock of Ages".

"Rock Of Ages"

1 Rock of Ages, cleft for me, Let me hide myself in Thee; Let the water and the blood, From Thy wounded side which flowed, be of sin the double cure, Save from wrath and make me pure.

2 Not the labor of my hands can fulfill Thy law's demands; Could my zeal no respite know, Could my tears forever flow, All for sin could not atone; Thou must save, and Thou alone.

3 Nothing in my hand I bring, Simply to Thy cross I cling; Naked, come to Thee for dress; Helpless, look to Thee for grace; Foul, I to the fountain fly; Wash me, Savior, or I die.

"Rock Of Ages"

4 While I draw this fleeting breath, when my eyes shall close in death, When I soar to worlds unknown, see Thee on Thy throne, Rock of Ages, cleft for me, let me hide myself in Thee.

"Blessed Beyond Measure"

This final hymn is not hundreds of years old; in fact, it was written only forty short years ago. Angela Spackman was living in the U.K. before the Lord lay on her and her husband's heart to come to America. She had just had her first baby girl Rachel. Although Angie and her husband Pete faced many difficulties and hardships her heart was full of gratitude as she looked down at her newborn daughter lying peacefully asleep in the crib. As she watched her one thought could not escape her mind, she was blessed beyond measure! Her heart overwhelmed with this thought, she found the only paper available and penned a beautiful song of worship and thanksgiving. The Spackman family were invited to minister many times at both Churches and the prisons in America. Then in 1987, the Spackman family moved to the U.S to continue doing ministry in the prisons. As they ministered to the inmates, their hearts became burdened for the inmates' children as well. They knew that without intervention, many of these children would become inmates themselves. Stepping out in faith and without any government

"Blessed Beyond Measure"

funding, they began a ministry right in their own home. Over the next several years, miracle after miracle took place! Although God provided every need along the way, it wasn't long before the Spackman's home became too crowded. However, once again God showed up; 18 acres of land in Alabama were donated to the ministry, and on that piece of land God provided for buildings to be built to house the children and give them a place of refuge. The Adullam House was the name the Lord laid on the Spackman's heart to call their ministry. In the Bible, David in 1 Samuel 22 was running for his life from King Saul. With nowhere to go, David found refuge in a cave called Adullam. In the same way, that David found refuge and a place of rest, the children at the Adullam house also find refuge and rest in a place filled with the love of God and the presence of the Holy Spirit. As I close this book out, I want you to read these powerful words penned by Mrs. Angie Spackman... "Blessed Beyond Measure"!

"Blessed Beyond Measure"

1 All that I am and own to this hour
I owe it to Jesus, to Calvary's power
I am blessed beyond measure and the
valleys seem small when compared to the
hilltops surrounding them all I am…

Chorus
Blessed beyond measure full to the brim,
Of mercy and goodness, all glory to him!
Who has saved me and kept me, and
new every day are the blessing he
showers my way!

2 The children he gave me, the husband
I love, the home that I live in, the friends
that I have. All these he has given and
none could deny, my cup runneth over
and I don't know why I am…

"Blessed Beyond Measure"

3 Oh Lord, let me bless you, as you have blessed me, with a life given over completely to thee. To spend, and be spent Lord, to give and not receive, is the least I can offer for I do believe I am...

Chorus
Blessed beyond measure full to the brim, Of mercy and goodness, all glory to him! Who has saved me and kept me, and new every day are the blessing he showers my way!

We encourage you to support the
Adullam House ministry on a full-time
basis! More information can be found on
their Facebook page or on their website:
adullamhouse.org

About The Author

Rev. Mark Munter was raised in Beaumont, Texas at an old-fashioned Pentecostal Church under the late Pastor B.H Clendennen. From a young age, he felt the call of God on his life to one day preach the gospel. At the age of 15, he surrendered his life at an altar to Jesus. It was there he first received the calling to preach. From there he began preaching in his youth group and in a bible club he had started at his High School. At the age of 18, he preached his first Youth Revival in Philadelphia, Pennsylvania, and there felt God birth the calling to minister to teens. After graduating High School, the door opened for him to attend Pastor David Wilkerson's (Founder of Teen Challenge and Times Square Church) Bible College in Pennsylvania. After graduating from Mt. Zion, Mark became a licensed minister and served in various ministry capacities preaching and serving part-time. In 2013, while in Louisiana, Mark found the love of his life and married Jamie shortly after. Together they stepped into full-time youth ministry in 2014. Later that same year they had their first child Melanie. In 2017 Mark received his Ordination with the Assemblies of God, and together with his family began pastoring. He is also the author of the books: *"Tough Questions and Biblical Answers"* and *"Countdown to Revelation"*

Made in United States
North Haven, CT
17 December 2022

29242428R00065